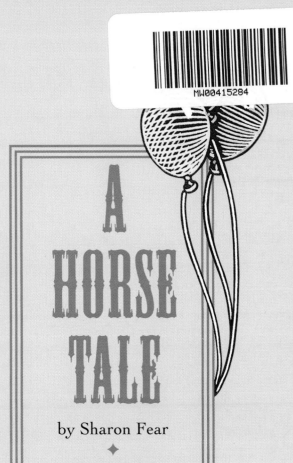

A HORSE TALE

by Sharon Fear

✦

illustrated by
Brad Teare

Scott Foresman

Editorial Offices: Glenview, Illinois • New York, New York
Sales Offices: Reading, Massachusetts • Duluth, Georgia
Glenview, Illinois • Carrollton, Texas • Menlo Park, California

I hate to tell this story. For one thing, it shows me up for what I am. Less than perfect, I guess you'd say.

But when other folks tell the tale, they always get it wrong. So . . . here's what REALLY happened.

I walked into town that morning to see the big show. The Circus Sabatini was here for just two days. And, being a bright and energetic fellow, I had a free pass. I'd earned it. I'd helped to feed and water the animals when the show arrived the day before.

But there was no show. There was just an
empty tent.

There were no lights. There was no music.
Not a man, woman, or child was around.

4

On the other hand, there was a mighty big commotion over by the courthouse. So I ran on over to see what all the fuss was.

"What is it?" I asked. "What's happened?"

"The circus people are on trial," said a lady.

"What for?" I asked. "What did they do?"

"They stole a horse," said a fellow nearby. "I thought you knew, Jeremiah. They stole Daisy, your Aunt Bonnie's horse."

"My . . . my aunt's horse!"

I just about choked.

Quick as I could, I plunged right through the crowd. I pushed my way into the courtroom.

People on the jury were snarling, shouting, and shaking their fists.

The sheriff was yelling at everyone. "Stop that yelling, or I'll stop it for you!"

The judge was banging away with his gavel. "Order! Order in this courtroom!" he cried.

A miner named Bob was on the stand. And so was his burro.

Up front sat Professor Sabatini in his scarlet coat and shiny top hat. He was waving a hanky at the judge. He was trying to get his attention.

Behind him sat the World's Strongest Man. His muscles bulged something fierce, probably with anger. Captain Courage, the lion tamer, coiled and uncoiled his whip.

And speaking of coiled. . . . the Snake Lady was wearing part of her act around her neck.

"Judge!" I cried. "Your Honor!"

But he couldn't hear me in all that racket.

"Quiet!" shouted the judge. "I'm trying to listen to evidence up here!"

"Now, Bob," said the judge, "you say that you saw the horse in question yesterday?"

"Yes, Your Honor. She was behind the circus tent. She was tied up to an animal cage. It was Daisy, all right. I know Daisy, and so does Zack here. Right, boy?"

"Eeee-YAW!" said the burro.

Well, I couldn't stand this any longer. You see, I knew something important. The Sabatinis weren't guilty! So I tried again.

"Judge, PLEASE!"

Next thing I knew, I was out in the street.
That judge was always a man of his word.

"Okay," I said out loud. "You want
evidence? You'll get evidence!"

I picked myself up and dusted off the seat
of my pants. Then I set off at a smart pace. I
had to get over to the circus grounds, quick!

When I led that zebra into the courtroom, no one tried to stop me. Then I threw water on it and started to scrub.

Well, eyes popped and jaws dropped.

Underneath was Daisy.

"Now, listen, all of you," I pleaded. "I'm to blame for this whole mess."

I explained how yesterday, over at the circus, the zebra got loose. It just ran clean away!

"Oooh," said the sheriff.

"The zebra pulls the clown wagon. The Professor said the act is nothing without that zebra. He said he might have to cancel the show!"

"Oh, no!" said several folks.

"But I got this idea," I said. "Aunt Bonnie lets me borrow Daisy anytime, without even asking!"

"Absolutely true, Your Honor," said Aunt Bonnie.

"So I suggested that my aunt's horse could pull that wagon. We could even paint stripes on her, like the zebra."

"Aha!" said several jurors.

"The Sabatinis weren't sure," I said. "But I reminded them of that great circus tradition: The show must go on!"

"That's right!" said the judge.

"So," I said. "About this horse-stealing charge . . . ."

"Not guilty!" cried the jury.
"Case dismissed!" cried the judge.
"Circus tonight!" cried the Sabatinis.
"Daisy, Daisy," said my aunt.
"Whew!" I said to myself.

Then everyone came rushing up, crowding around the Sabatinis. Everyone was slapping them on the back. People were saying how glad they were that the Sabatinis wouldn't have to go to jail. People were asking for the Sabatinis' autographs. People were buying tickets for the show.

And that reminds me. Daisy played her part really well that night. As for whatever happened to the real zebra. . . .

Well, nobody knows for sure. But, from
time to time, you do hear stories!